Wasteful Money: *What's in your pocket*

Bobby Simonds

https://bobbysimonds.co

Copyright © 2019 Bobby Simonds

All rights reserved. No part of this publication may be reproduced, distributed, or transmitted in any form or by any means, including photocopying, recording, or other electronic or mechanical methods, without the prior written permission of the publisher, and/or author, except in the case of brief quotations embodied in critical reviews and certain other noncommercial uses permitted by copyright law. For permission requests, email **bobby.simonds@gmail.com** . Serious inquiries only.

ISBN: **9781706941309**

ISBN 13: **XXXXX**

Library of Congress Control Number: **XXXXX**

LCCN Imprint Name: **Independently published**

https://bobbysimonds.com/

Any references to historical events, real people, or places are, used fictitiously. Names, characters, & places are products of the author's imagination.

Front Cover & Editing by author.

bobby.simonds@gmail.com

www.facebook.com/bobbyrsimonds

www.instagram.com/@bobbysimonds

#bobbyraysimonds

#bobbysimonds

#BOBBYRAYSIMONDS

#ATWISTINTRAVEL

#risenfromtheashes

#toxicamerica

#Challenge-thyself

#avoidinghavoc

#bobbyscreativephotographyseries

#QUESTIONINGREALITY

#thedoctorscall

#evilmatters

#pandorasbox

#everythingchangeswithbrainsurgery

#therealjerrylewis

#wastefulmoney

From the Author:

I want to thank you ahead of time for your interest in this book, and others that you may read/purchase. Please be kind, and leave me a review after you finish, this book. Thanks again!

About the author:

As a self-taught author, and photographer, I spend much time researching many various topics. This could very well include current events, current conspiracies, and current conspiracy gossip (which I put a spin on that name).

Between using Google & Youtube; one could easily lose themselves in this long, and eventful lavish web.

I have created/published many books; which with my nonfiction, I have more than enough proof, which I can not only keep up with current events, but years later, my books seem to stay up-to-date.

Like many authors before me, I too, am exceptionally observant. I am also intrigued with the successful, mindset of being an international author, and as I continue to write, my books become more successful because of people like you, who took a chance on something new, and original to read!

I was born with Mild Cerebral Palsy, and have had brain surgery. Which, I do not allow either to slow me down, and/or get in my way. I do not compare myself to other authors, however, I do believe I have what it takes.

Booklovers connect with me from my own personal biography. Connecting with readers on more of an emotional level; I decided to include topics such as: inner healing, conspiracy, grievance, political, suicide, & finishing up with positive outcomes.

On a side note, I have assisted others to glorify their dream, by directing them with the essentials for writing, and the publishing tools, that they would need, of course.

I've soared over topics such as, social media, "fake news," UFOs, the Alien Conspiracy, "mythical" creatures, religion, politics, cloning, life-sucking tablets. Furthermore, in one book, I even predicted Donald Trumps' win, before he was even close to upsetting Hilary Clinton's supporters.

As far as my fiction books go, I must say that I am still in the process of enjoying a world to create for my readers to escape their normal bubble, to enjoy somebody else's insanity. I currently only have one true novel, and the rest being, labeled as 'novella's' or short stories. Majority of my books, both fiction & nonfiction, generally are series. Obviously, I wrote a few individuals, but I prefer the other choice.

I hope that you are brave enough to leave your review of what you had thought of with this book, and others. Whether you are a previous supporter of mine, or a new one, be respectful and leave a review where you had purchased this book. Thanks for your participation, and I look forward to reading your review, or messages to me.

In addition, I hope you (the reader) check back on Amazon.com (or whatever link you purchased my titles), monthly, because I tend to publish a minimum of 5 books per year. Majority of the time, it's more realistically 10 books per year. And on a super good year, it's like two books

per month! Imagine that!

WASTEFUL CHANGE

Did you realize, in just New York State alone, by not returning your recyclable cans and bottles, that those nickels add up to roughly: seventeen thousand dollars a year? And did you also know, that the people that work in those departments (for the redemption – state employees) split the $17k per year as a bonus? I bet you didn't, because I just learned about it, and never realized that it goes into somebody's pocket!

Like many people (like myself), we don't think about things such as a nickel going into somebody's pocket, just because we didn't get our nickels back…

Another wasteful area with change, is when you have a few pennies up to a quarter left over from a gas station. Many people often flick a penny (to even a quarter) into the "give a penny" holder, which lies on the counter, next to the clerk. If not used for the following customer, it goes into the gas owner's pocket, and with the shady employees, into theirs!

When I worked at a gas station [which had slot machines for the casino – a.k.a., the Turning Stone Casino], people would leave the printed tickets with pennies, and on up to a buck. You must realize it doesn't go into the trash can, nor does it go to the employee – as many assumed so, when I worked there. In fact, it goes straight back to the 'head-honcho's' pocket at the end of the year. I learned that it was often tallied up to around the low, hundreds of thousands of dollars – per year! All from just leaving pennies and a buck on a printed ticket. Trust me, if you are in need [or know somebody who may need it], it's best to cash it in, and just hand it over to them (or the clerk, in the tip container).

A wiseman once told me (my beloved, deceased Grandfather), *"Lose change can add up, that's how we {him & his wife} took vacations every year."*

If you don't like change, as many seem to be having a dislike with in the past few years, then keep your change in a five-gallon water jug. When it fills, gift it to somebody, who needs the money. Everyone knows someone who is going thru a rough patch. Nobody that goes thru that rough patch, enjoys watching you throw your money away!

UNHEALTHY DONATIONS

I have mentioned in many prior books about the pointless donations that exist in today's society. It's insane to think, that there are many people who truly don't understand how the world works – even the elderly!

Nonetheless, when it comes to donating to a cause,' people don't research other options – especially, when it's a health-related issue.

As far as the "Cancer Society" is concerned, **STOP** donating to them. There was a cure for cancer back in the

1960s. It was created in Canada, and was rejected by majority (if not all) countries, internationally.

Why, you may ask?

It's a simple explanation, really. It's because ***fighting cancer is expensive***. If there were millions of people who were cured before all the so-called treatment methods, used today, there wouldn't be "research centers" for "curing cancer." Because, they already have, as I stated. It's not fiction, it's fact. Just Google-it!

There are millions of wasted dollars going for Cancer donations, for "research." It's one of the biggest donation scams, I've ever come across.

Majority of any illness donations are a scam, created both by the Governments and Health Administrations. If everyone wasn't sick, there'd only be surgical centers and Emergency Buildings. Because, they wouldn't need to place a doctor's office in every town/city in every state, providence, or country internationally. Just think of the billions, if not trillions of dollars wasted in medical care. Not to mention, they're run by 'scientists.' The same scientists that guess ninety percent of the time, when they come across something that they didn't have to memorize out of a book from medical school!

I generally get a good laugh when I see advertisements for "BLOOD SHORTAGES."

You're telling us that 'you' are suddenly short on blood, when there are hundreds of thousands of people donating blood in any given month? This tells me that "they" are planning something big, like a so-called natural disaster that hasn't occurred, quite yet – or one that has literally just happened. They have enough blood in their storage to last the next fifty years, I guarantee you! Unreal!

Disability Research is another scheme created in the medical field. If one were to do any basic research, many disabilities are man-made created – just like all diseases.

With my born-disability, *Mild Cerebral Palsy*, there isn't a cure (at least for adults). It has always been geared toward assisting children with it, but as soon as you turn 18, your shit-out-of-luck to have any type of assistance. The reasoning, is because there's more to gain (as a medical "professional"), with constant co-payments, and in some cases, surgery. They've come a long way since I was born, but again, there is absolutely no assistance for when you become an adult. More than most doctors in the area (in Upstate N.Y.) don't even know what it is, unless you're in a wheel chair. Unbelievable! Even the court system cracks jokes, because it's a non-visual disability.

And for those of you unfamiliar with Mild Cerebral Palsy, in the first place, the simplistic way to describe it is as follows: weak muscles, tiredness (and easily tired), lack of mobility, muscles don't fully develop in mostly legs, arms, & back. It also affects the brain, such as, memory, comprehensive skills, some motor functions, sex drive – yes – and even the ability to focus and retain information. This is all just for the Mild Cerebral Palsy conditions. Therefore, if you know somebody with C.P. that is in a wheelchair, it's like a vegetable, with some alertness, but not much. Those people I feel sorry for, because it's no way to live. If I were like them, I'd want to hit the "restart-button" on my life – or "end-here!"

Furthermore, if you see the ***Cerebral Palsy Donation Research Center***, think twice, because unless you know how your money will be spent, it's pointless. If it's only to help the children, what about the adults?

Down Syndrome is another wasteful donation, because they, again, created this disability, and there has been a large spike in New York State alone since 2014. The numbers are staggering, and in 2014 it was something like 2% of the population in the state, and its gone up to 14 or 18% by 2018. It's something close to those numbers. I cannot be exact, so don't sue me! (LOL)

AUTISM is another man-made creation. This isn't something that occurs at birth, however. This disability is caused by ingredients that are in house cleaning chemicals – that aren't generally labeled for the consumers awareness. I learned about this in 2018 while watching documentaries about the discrepancies that are used in the dyes of clothing, household cleaning products, and other various things. It was well-documented, I wish I wrote down the title of the documentary, because it was alarming.

People that fall victim to Autism are generally between 2-6 years old. Majority of the time, it's noticed by somebody you know, and occasionally, by your child's doctor. But majority of the time, they don't say anything to the parent, unless they're a good doctor! Sorry to say, but it's true.

And if Autism is caught early on, there isn't a cure, but there are specialized schools currently that will at least help the development for the child, before entering 'real' school-life. My youngest nephew has it, and what a difference with the specialized school. Just be patient, because they have an extra dose of stubbornness that is thrown into the temper-tantrums, that you've gotta ride it out!

Again, if you were considering donating for Autism, make sure it goes for education purposes only, because there isn't anything the medical departments want to do with such a disability.

The dyes in clothing are generally itchy, right? Well, I learned that there's a deeper reasoning behind the itchiness. It's because it has a chemical that is harmful to both children and adults, which is suppose to seep into the skin. By doing so, it becomes another 'unknown' disease, which can create disabilities, such as Autism over a short period of time.

Just like the clothing dyes, household chemicals carry hidden chemicals that don't always show up on the ingredients listed. Because, the companies declare that if they print their 'secret' ingredient, any interested party could create their product. Therefore, by law, they get the exception. It's a gray area, but generally if most cleaning products were tested, it would be highly toxic, as I learned from multiple videos that I had viewed since 2018.

With harmful toxins that are used in our daily household lives, the companies that provide such products know we – the consumer – won't stand and read the warning/ingredient labels. And, even if we do, we won't know what the hell we're even reading, because it's generally words that we've never heard of – or know the meaning of. They know this, and I guarantee you, like the medical field & scientific communities, they create new words that are confusing to the masses – that we are like, *can't you just speak our language, already?*

This is the main reason why these companies get away with majority of the crap they get away with!

In the past year or two, Facebook has created a page or 'celebration' for donations. You can now pick from a vast selection for donations, and many people are doing this for their birthdays…*scratching my head*

The bottom line, is that you must make damn certain where your donations are going. What companies are in control of the donations. And research it, first.

Wealthy people seem to think if they donate millions to a hospital, that they will have priority, with the best healthcare, if they ever themselves, land in the hospital. I'm certain they get priority. However, doctor's will be doctor's. It's like the saying goes, *Technology is only as good as the dumbass using it.* Therefore, they can lay out a strategic battle plan, but if you have cancer, you will die, I'm sorry. It's a fact. If they don't cure it for the little guy, they won't provide you with the cure, suddenly. They'll take your money, and laugh at you behind closed doors, just like the rest of us…

LOST ADVANCES

In the 1950s there were many advertisements, television shows (such as the cartoon series, *The Jetsons*), and talk about automobiles without tires! They in fact created vehicles that hovered. The technology was in fact, created, but never launched.

If you do simple research on Google, as I do, just to get to the basics, you will eventually come across a magazine article, with a picture of a 1950s, convertible Cadillac that was in red and white, that hovered. It was, quite neat. But the technology was denied, because of manufactures that would lose billions and trillions of dollars.

It was all about the oil industries, that would be losing all the money. Therefore, they leaped, fought, and came out on top, obviously. This was also about a decade before the invention of using fossil fuels instead of gasoline. Another deniability from the Oil Industries.

With the hovering vehicle concept, it was supposed to be way less costly to the consumer, and better for the environment. Obviously, money talks, when it comes to trillions of dollars that the oil industries knew they'd be at a loss.

Credit card companies are a huge scam, in my opinion. Yes, I had a few when I turned 18 (years ago). Nevertheless, between the interest, and the money you must pay back, it doesn't do much for the person who has a credit card – except for a short/large advance of money that doesn't exist, until you pay the bill, with money you generally don't have, to begin with.

People are under the impression that by gaining access to a credit card, it will significantly assist your credit score. In fact, it does little to nothing, unless you have a huge credit line.

The bottom line is this: *If you cannot afford it, don't buy it.*

The purpose isn't helping your credit score get better these days, it's all about getting you further into debt!

The best way to go, if you're trying to raise your credit score would be mortgages & car loans. The shorter the loan –

generally 2-3 years – the better the results. Just don't default!

Gambling can lead to addiction, like drugs or alcohol. Nevertheless, people that win under $600 don't have to claim taxes upon their winnings. However, even though you are using your *already taxed money*, anything over $600 is taxed, and taxed high. Therefore, is it worth the headache?

Furthermore, if you are gambling daily, weekly, or monthly, how much are you wasting, while attempting to hit the jackpot, that is a 1 and a million odds?

There are many people who gamble with the little income that they have with hoping to be the next ***LUCKY WINNER***! How much are you losing? How much are you willing to lose, before gaining anything? You're wasting your money, and it's not an intelligent way to attempt to become a millionaire!

WASTEFUL SERVICES

There is a long list of services that shouldn't exist, but they do. I'm obviously not going to go over very many, as I'm cutting this book to around 100 pages; plus, I don't want to bore you!

One of the main wasteful services in my opinion, however, would have to be EDITING. If you have a computer, and you are using Microsoft Word, or something similar, you already have editing software imbedded. MS Word is the best, obviously (thank you Microsoft).

Therefore, stop spending thousands on Editing services.

With my first novel, "A twist in travel: Fate," I spent an incredible $1,375. And let me just say, it wasn't worth it, except for get the: © , for the copyright page. Nevertheless, it's a waste of money. Imagine, if I had paid for editing services for every book I've published, it would be around $100k. That's insane, when all things considered, I don't make much from sales. Therefore, not all investments are worthwhile.

Book covers can be a good investment if you don't have the capabilities with doing so, but it's an easy thing to do if you are self-publishing thru Amazon. They already have the software, and often pictures to choose from – just an FYI, they don't take down a picture after you select it. Therefore, if you use one of their pictures for your cover, you may not be the only one using it! Annoying, right?

Wasteful Hope

There are many organizations that expect weak people – who hope for change – that will automatically donate their, hard-earned money. And, in many cases, they parade around the weak, gaining vast amounts of wealth.

One such organization that comes to mind, is Organized Religion. How often do people donate their money on any given attendance? There are those that show up every Sunday (some churches in mid-week services), the holiday attendees, and the ones that go once or twice a year.

Nevertheless, if you show up to church, everyone is familiar with the "passing of the basket" concept.

Churches such as, Saddleback Church, in Mission Viejo, California, not only went from renting out a space at Trabuco Hills High School in the basketball court inside, to such a vast space, just up the road from the school. It's beyond what the pastors had ever anticipated when they began raising money for such a church. It's one of the largest churches I've ever seen, and it's not a Roman Catholic Church! It's Christianity.

I was amazed how quickly the church grew, in only a short few years. It's impressive, and the last time I had gone was with my mother, Christmas of 2005. They literally did "the passing of the basket" per row; by using only one basket to fill a row, mind you. They may have well passed a money bucket, because there were some, who strongly believed to give ten percent of their weekly earnings to the church – because that is what is written in the Bible. Yes, 10%! That's nuts.

Especially, when you have those whom believe the more they donate, the stronger their belief becomes that they are purchasing their spot in Heaven! How foolish, right? It sounds like selling your soul to God. Just as some believe selling their soul to the devil for fortune and fame…Just revealing my comparison!

With that all said, and yeah, I said it! It proves my point, with some churches, that they parade religion around the weak and hopeful. Was it always this way? Why does it seem as though I'm the only individual that notices their games?

I have also realized this with the freshly recruit's for joining the military branches. Just out of high school, not even a week, they'll be at the movies with their friends, and become a victim of the bombardment with advertisements with joining any given military branch. All because they make it sound hopeful, prideful, and adventurous. Pride, shmm.

Forcing young American's to give their lives to "Defend America" for wars they have no business joining. Resources that shouldn't be spent, nor black body bags and coffins that are sent back, because they – the government suits – feel nothing when losing thousands of lives on the battlefield, defending oil, killing innocent people overseas, just because of their religion.

Don't get me wrong, I support our troops 100%. What I don't support is the mindless wars that our American Government stirs up for monetary gain. And it's not just the government, because what we're all taught in the workforce, is that you always have somebody higher than you, to answer to (unless you own your own company). And since the

American Government doesn't technically own America, well, they answer to somebody else, who forces our governments hand in making decisions and placing the American People to blame the President. Therefore, think twice about blaming Trump for everything that you assume he has done wrong. He's done a lot more than the past few so-called POTUS's.

It's only Money

People that say, "it's only money," drive me up the wall. I hear it more often than one would guess.

Nevertheless, the people that say that, have never been truly broke. They aren't generally the one's who have to figure out how to survive between paychecks. They make enough money to cover all their bills, plus waste their money with tossing their change aside, as though the change isn't money!

I for one, can let you know, it's not just money, it's a source to survive with.

Without money, we'd all be screwed in the modern era, where money is everything.

I used to say, "money is everything." I suppose I still do. Nevertheless, it is everything. To ever get anywhere in life, money is an necessity. It purchases everything we need to live out our lives. It pays our bills. It pays for our food. It pays for our homes. It pays for our unnecessary entertainment. It pays for our grooming. It pays for our hygiene. It pays for our vehicles. It pays. It pays. It pays!

It is quite offense to here, "money isn't everything." Because, it is everything. Without it, we'd be homeless, and starving.

To get ahead in life, we also need money. Money to pay for our websites, advertisements, and business cards. It may seem pointless to many, but to the many it seems pointless to, they don't have what it takes to make a difference.

When I go on job interviews (since becoming an author), I must hold back the laughter when they read my resume, and say, "oh, you're an author?" They always act interested at first, but always assume that there isn't much to the artistry of being an author. It takes many hardships to push yourself to ever get out of the gutter with anything. But being an author, well, it can be worse than trying to make it as a musician. You must set aside everything, to strive to be the best in your field. Becoming noticed is next to impossible, unless of course, you have connections. When living in Upstate New York, it seems that Publishers just assume you are part of "dumb farmer community." But they're wrong. Creating, editing, designing, for the long haul, isn't an easy task. Selling is next to impossible, too.

The bottom line is, authors aren't lazy. They must put in a ton of blood, sweat, and tears, to focus on their end-game. Which, isn't so much as becoming the next best-seller. Moreover, it's about being noticed by traditional publishers, along with the masses.

Especially, since we live in time, that people assume that authors that self-publisher their work online, should give their books away for free...?! It's still a business, that we cannot afford to give our books away for free. Setting them to ninety-nine cents, is below what we'd like to promote them for. Especially, if you would consider how much time a book could take us to create, edit, and publish. Then, with many authors, the time and money it takes them to advertise. And, you want *free* books? We cannot afford to offer free books, because we'll never get ahead, or break even.

If you are one of those whom believe an author should give away their books for free…Just consider working for free for your job…It doesn't sound like something you would do, does it? We don't work for free, it's just another form of ***Wasteful Money***.

Wasteful Money Tips

If you google *wasteful money*, there are a ton of links/threads that pop up in less than two seconds.

One list that caught my eye, however, was about ATM fees. That's no joke. Especially, if you are just doing a balance inquiry at an ATM that isn't attached to your bank. This costs you about 50 cents. When you take money out, that's generally around $2.50 plus your own bank fee, added on top of that charge. I only recommend that action, when it's absolutely, necessary.

For those vacationers, that's a whole other fee, you don't want to spend, unless it's a must.

I remember back in 2001, I was visiting Upstate New York, when I resided in California. I went to pull out $300, and it literally cost me $20, between the ATM and my bank! I was only planning on withdrawing $100, but to make it worth it, $300 sounded more reasonable!

Because, the issue with many smaller places, such as diners, they don't accept credit cards, or bank cards – which forces you to use cash. Back in 2001, there were even bars that would only accept cash, what a shock that was!

Rental car insurance is another waste, because if you already have car insurance, it covers a rental car! And, your own car insurance already has your rates imbedded. Such being, the deductible upon an accident. With car rental insurance, your deductible could be as low as $1000. Which, most policies are $500.

One lesson we've learned with purchasing a used car in the past, is the so-called *extended warranty* from the small dealership! What a waste of money that document is. Especially, if you live in a place like Upstate New York, and are constantly worrying about rust/rot from underneath your car, when purchasing a used car. Rot is no joke in this area. You can cover up majority of the beginning stages of rot, simply by using black spray paint. And if you aren't a mechanic, 9 times out of 10, you won't even see it, until you purchase it, and it wears off a few months later.

The horrible thing about getting screwed on these so-called warranties, is that it automatically voids any warranties, based on rot. Therefore, 99% of used vehicles that are over six years old, and is low to the ground, generally has rot somewhere – you can get lucky, but most times not. Therefore, that added two thousand dollars you didn't really want to spend extra on, because it was taking the rest of your money, well…You may have guess it already – you just got swindled…legally!

Credit Card interest can be a killer too, which creates wasteful money. I had three credit cards in my life, back when I was nineteen. It seems like an automatic approval when you graduate high school! It's sad. Anyway, my first one was a Texaco card, with a limit of $100. It seemed low, but at the time, it only cost me $30 for a carton of cigarettes (which here the cheapest is $75 and as high as $150!); and a gas fill-up was under $10! The good ol' days.

Therefore, a $100 credit limit was reasonable, back then. Either way, my interest was low, but the late fees were improbable. At first it was only ten dollars, then they sky-rocketed after the first six months to $45. That was nuts. By my second credit card (Mastercard), I was in a heap of crap! The credit limit was (if I recall correctly) around $500. At the time, I was between jobs. Therefore, the five hundred dollars went fast, and it was the beginning of a long line of credit debt. It took me three years and a ton of headaches and screaming and melt-downs talking with them, to come to terms with a proper payment plan. That was the worst collection agent I ever dealt with.

Ten years after that crap, I got my last credit card, with Best Buy. The credit limit on that, was also $500. Two items later, I lost my job, and couldn't pay them back. I ignored the calls, and letters in the mail, and it was written off, a year later.

The point of my story with credit cards, is there are a ton of people like me who think they can get items with credit cards, when, they (me), cannot afford these items in the first place.

Over seventy percent of American's are currently in debt. Many have credit cards, or get bank loans to cover products that they shouldn't be purchasing. Because now, you are furthering your debt, and you are giving people jobs, to collect funds, you cannot afford because of no financial security, through your current job!

The Bottom Line

Think twice about wasteful money. Loose change is still currency…save it you think you don't want to carry it, rather than placing it inside of a store, throwing it on the ground, etc.

Stop saying, *it's only money*. You will offend somebody, who can't make ends meet. If you feel that way, start donating your money to poor people, they can use it!

Thanks for reading, and don't forget to leave a review where you purchased your copy.

https://bobbysimonds.com/

www.ingramcontent.com/pod-product-compliance
Lightning Source LLC
Chambersburg PA
CBHW030941240526
45463CB00015B/886